My Seeking Spirit

being free variations on
poems by Kalidasa
c. 500 A.D.

by

HAROLD MORLAND

Privately Printed
1966

Further copies may be obtained from:

Printed by Gibbs & Sons, Orange Street, Canterbury

NOTE

Scholars in his language have called Kalidasa 'the Shakespeare of Sanskrit literature'.

This makes my arrogance in presenting these 'variations' the more astounding. His long poem THE CYCLE OF THE SEASONS bears, perhaps, the same relation to his major work as Shakespeare's sonnets do to ANTHONY AND CLEOPATRA, or to LEAR. I am in no position to judge.

Indeed, it would be insolent in me to pretend that the short poems that follow are in *any* sense a translation. They are 'variations on an Indian theme'. They have as much 'reality' as an album of snapshots in comparison with the vibrant magnificence of the great Hindu temples. They must be regarded merely as snapshots. For one thing, the unity of Kalidasa's poem is destroyed. Think of the carvings in the Louvre, where a few statues are offered as works of art, when their purpose and place was a moment of worship in a great cathedral of belief. So, at best, these lyrics are the memories of an experiencing mind.

Kalidasa's theme is the wholeness of life. My versions are simple variations on that theme.

H.M.

THE SEASONS ROUND

SUMMER

I

The hot, hot days return
  With the sun on fire;
But a delicate moon in the night
  On the mirroring pool
Shivers with quick delight
  As we dive into cool
Kissing water, hissing where we burn,
  Quenching the embers of desire.

Night's deep umber is barred
  With slivers of silver;
The palace lies open, bared
  To the fingering breeze . . .
To the syllable-murmuring streams that lip
  A soft name, and slip
Through a maze of flowers . . .
                            and wheels that raise
  The water clank, then drowse.
                                    These
And the jewel-gleams, the stars' cool fire,
  Return, my love, return
  For your desire.

Strange with elusive lights
  The palace quivers;
And a perfume floats
  Like wine
That under quiet breathing wavers;
  Music pulses, and the notes
  Tremble up to the divine . . .
Now, oh now is the hour of lovers.

4

The fevers of Summer thicken
  The blood in my veins—
You can assuage it, quicken
  Relief with the Rains,
Charm-weaving girl whose loins
Are in clouds of silk, whose nipples
  —With sandal sweet—
    Are set in pearl,
Whose hair with fragrance flows, whose feet,
  Curved like a rippling stream,
    Bear rings that chime
Like the song of a rose flamingo, and their lines
    Upward dream.

5

Let me grow weary with woman, whose breast
  With crimson sandal is wet,
  Whose garment of pearl sways
  With jasmine scenting its fold;
    To be wearier yet
    I raise
    Love's crest
  To take her haunches girt with gold.

6

She sheds her robe from proud
  Assertive breasts, oh quick
    Her body endowed
With statements only of truth
  In the candour of youth.

7

Fans that softly kiss the air
    Awake;
  Guitar that gently weeps;
    A far
Calling bird—and love that sleeps
  Till glances break from out her eyes
    At moonrise.

8

  As in the palace, deep
  With sleep their only veil
The lovers lie—the moon, still white
With shame, whispers their tale
  And now the night
    Grows pale.

Hot dust blinds the eye
Of the wanderer whose lust
Makes his heart dry;
"Will there be water", cry the deer
"At the wood's edge?"—their fear
Searching the sky.

The limp snake fails,
And her chin falls
In the fiery dust. Forgetting hate,
She lies in the shade
Of the peacock's tail, displayed
That the feathers may vibrate.

The breathless lion is dying;
Birds pant on the drooping trees;
The buffaloes, their muzzles thick
With a hot spume, are lying
Where the lake is all uneasy slime;
The shrivelled grasshoppers have fallen
On the baked earth of that last cistern.

12

We are afraid. We are afraid. One flower
Blooms there, past the parching fields,
Scattering its golden pollen in a shower
　　Till the whole forest yields
　　A crop no farmer could desire . . .
The trees will set the very sky afire.

13

Leaping and hungry it crunches
　　The writhing branches
And juicy lianas; and the grasses
Swither and hiss as it passes.
Trunk after trunk, the great trees crack
　　As it raises with its might
A fan of wind. It roars out its delight
　As the maddened beasts lose track
　　Of themselves, and kin and kind,
　　And blunder to the riverbed.

But the mud reflects that red.

14

A lion with a flickering mane,
A monkey screaming with the pain
Of its burnt paws; a leaping deer—
And all with one hot, linking fear;
As enemies in the face of death
With only prayer exhaust their breath.

15

But to you—my dear, dear friend—
Long nights of love, that end
    In a quiet sleep;
And a moon that seems to linger
Only that her long white finger
    Can delicately reveal
Some half-forgotten treasure
For your new-roused body's pleasure.

Then, like the hungry Lord of Fire,
You'll burn the night with your desire.

THE SEASON OF RAINS

1

Like elephants in rut, whose loins
    Are overcharged, the clouds
Advance—enormous, full of rain.

Like kings, when the battle joins
With thunder for drums and lightning-jags
    For the swift silk of their flags,
      Again and again
    They charge the ramparts of the mountain . . .
To be repelled into disordered crowds.

2

The clouds mass slowly over the plain
    Like the dark blue petals
  Of the lotus; like the full round breasts
    Of a nursing woman; and like fard
      On the face of the sky.

3

Then like an army dispersed and retreating
  The ceaseless patter, then heavier beating
  Of battalion-raindrops. And high
  —With the caution of an unsure ally—
    The peacocks raise their crests;
    And the desperate chataka-bird
      Lifts its gaping throat
      And sings a note unheard
      In praise of this
    Delirious armistice.

4

The red-tipped mushrooms burst from the dissembling
    Inhibition of the earth;
  The young grass-shoots are trembling
  With beads of lapis—their first toys.

  Like diamonds on a woman in the night
    Are the fireflies—golden shepherd-boys
      Of Indra. Quiet is delight.

5

The peacocks spread like flowers;
Then, at the ground-beat of the showers,
    They dip and begin to sway
And with a courtly pride display
Their grace and beauty. Seeing these,
    The marketing bees
    —Thinking them flowers indeed—
Alight, and bustle in a housewife greed.

6

The bloated rivers, bruised and blue
    As drunken harlots, rave
In their broken beds. They snatch the upright tree
    In the grip of a wave
To the salty death of the sea.

7

But the forest-pool is still, under the smells
Of flowers fretted only by gazelles.

8

On paths lit only by the silent flare
  Of summer lightning, women dare
  The watching night. And when they slip
  To a lover's bed, fearing the thunder,
They find new cause for trembling, under
  The secret safety of his thighs' hard grip.

9

But the lonely woman turns and twists
    On her unstained bed;
    She beats with her fitsts
  Her nipples that unwanted harden;
    And remembering other days
    Her fingers walk their ways
Through an unattended garden.

10

  How thick is the yellow flood
    That rolls along
Corpses of creatures, earth, and eddying trees
    In its strong
  And sullen anger. Like a rearing snake.
    The frog, in its deep throat, sees
  Devouring death, but cannot make
  That last wild leap from this quaking mud.

But the rocks are wet again
    With the kiss of the cloud;
The peacock lifts his head
    And begins to dance;
The pleasing whisper of the rain
Makes the shyest blossom proud
    Of the evening's quickened glance.

Who is unmoved, my love, is still unproved.
    Why should delight
    Wait for the go-between of night?

12

We are at one with nature. Rivers flow
And our blood too; the rustling rain
Is my fingers in your hair; the gleam
Of moistened leaves, your eyes that show
In the dusk. And heavily the fruit
Weighs in your hand.
                Two linked particulars
Of the worshipped and perfecting Absolute.

AUTUMN

1

The earth is covered with a blue lace
    Of flowering kashas, and the night
With a muslin of dew catches the light
        —Oh slight
    Over the slow drift and the grace
        Of the stream . . .
    The islands seem
                the roundness of sleeping thighs
        And the white birds on the shores
            Are pearls
        Delight has given to the girls . . .
            As to the wise
        The mind's unprompted metaphors.

2

The soil there—look!—is dusted
    With red pollen.
                Can't you hear
The very heart-beat in the stem that thrusted
    Up from its sleep?
                Who knows

—Which of us knows?—
The glory within the rose?
And shall our innocence suffice
To measure all the harvest in the rice?

3

The dark rebellion of the storm
Is over. Clouds are white
As the lacy fibres of a lotus-leaf,
And form
A fan to cool the coming royal night
Of the sky.
There's silver in the air.
And a flower's belief
Can silence any fool that's asking "Why".

4

The night, a ripening girl prepared
For delight, has bared
The innocent white
curve of her moon;
And round her throat are the stars.
Her whole dark beauty's thought
In particulars.
And her dress
Is this seen-through darkness
From the subtle silk of nought.

5

The kiss of the water.
                    And this
Red lotus, and even the shadows are stained
    With the blood's desire;
    And the banks that should lie
    With an artist's limning stillness
                    Stir
    And the birds—how quiet they were!—
            Are pained
    And restless, trivially enquire.
            But even in sleep
    The river in between flows deep.

6

    If I were lost from you,
                    you'd find me again
    In the quiet fall of the rain.

7

Listen.
      In the dark, can you not hear
—Not thinking we are near—
What little tales they tell each other,
Shy girl to girl, brother to boasting brother.

8

And we remember in your laughing faces
The joys that left their little traces.
      What lover lives without the stain
      And shining blemishes of pain?

Love is its own self's comfort, but not peace,
A prisoner praying never for release.

9

And Autumn here is sleeping on a swan
That moves over water of emerald glass;
      Or the night himself her oarsman
      Ferries her through the stars.

10

The rising sun.
                    The scarlet water-lily
Opens her lips like a young girl coming awake.

11

   Autumn be kind to you, my love, who smile
Where the lotus is white, and kiss
         Where it's red;
                         and the glistening dew
   Is the light of your eyes when I find the lotus blue.

WINTER

1

If in the winter,
                    if in white
The world is covered with a shame,
    And the same
Ripeness of harvest promises now
    Neither flower nor seed,
        Quietly we plead
            Not for delight
But answers to our When? and How?

2

    Fling gold away. Destroy this flaunting
Frippery of silk, and colours, and the ching
        Of bracelets. Birds don't sing
    In the heart of winter. Something haunting,
        Something without name—absurd,
            A word—
    Not seed, not flower, nor root . . . but the air
        Has eyes, has eyes that stare.

3

Look at me. I am wearied
With love.
                    Not "of" but "with" you.
Give me a sleeping winter to forgive you
     My blundering replies
  To where I know you're wise.
And yet I know my body's truth is queried.

4

As open as the fields they lie,
And still the curlews cry.

5

  Stay quiet by this pool. The leaves
Are kindly to the wind's scurry,
     As my green mind believes
That God is underneath the stillness of this hurry.

6

And yet I love you.
                    Water rippled by birds.
Your body's silence.
                    My clamouring words.

7

This dancing tree. This mango. Chorusing with
flowers
To the drumming kiss of showers,
This fingering beat, these fingers of the rain
This rain this rain this beat
Where it seems my spirit has cool feet
On the bodies bodies bodies of white flowers.

8

But her whole life long the swan restrains
The whiteness of her pains,
Until in autumn she can tear the sky
With one heaven-slitting cry.

9

Yet the quiet wind is dancing, dancing on the leaves,
And restless in their beds the girls
Listen, and maybe blame the silly
First gold-pollen shedding of the lily.

10

But have you seen the white breast of a swan that glides
Through waters, and creates its own dark tides?

11

Time is in love with us.

It brings in the rain
Its happiness, and with its kiss
Pleads that it can't explain
Minutes like this.

12

The sky is full of thousands of delight,
Yet some would think it all one night.

THE SEASON OF DEWS

I

The dew is cold. And this is the night,
    Star-heavy and alone.
   The terrace has a silver light
    But is cold stone.
  My clothes are suddenly thinned . . .
I feel not you, not you, but the wind.

2

Into this room, my love, into this room
    And the sleeping air
       Aware
  Of nothing more than lovers whom
  It sheathes in perfume and in silence there,
    Yet leaves them bare.

3

The dawn's too soon. But not my eyes
Complain against their sight,
   Just my two thighs
  Still blundering with delight.

4

They bathe with me in the river, these young men,
    And wash their bodies clean
Of the saffron-marks and all the heavy scent
      Of something "then" ...
    For nothing must be seen
      Of the one thing meant.

5

Defeated. In their manly pride
    They see this radiant bride
With the empire of her world require
    The endless tribute of desire.

6

And still you move, and still you stir the air
    And the stars surround you
      And my earth is where?
    Yet when I've found you
I need a time for patience, and for prayer.

7

Darkness delight you.
                But the whitening day
    Brings one truth only.
              Who shall say?

8

This time for tiredness. This hour
    Of the drooping flower
  Is praise of the heaviness of seed.
    And every time has need
Of its own blessing, blessing that it gives—
For the living dies, but also the dying lives.

9

Farmer of love, take even this crumbling earth
    And know its worth;
And feel inside its soil a beating birth.

10

  Dew on the rose.
              On every flower
Feed to the root its life and power.

SPRING

1

Look, my dear, it's spring. And on his bow
   Love stretches a string of bees,
      Each arrow
     Tipped with a scarlet mango bud,
      And sees
     Us as his trembling quarry.

2

This pool is spring,
This laughter of water
Is time's young daughter
With a jewelled plaything.

3

   Love is leaping in his rage,
     Panting to engage . . .
And the faces of the young he blesses
   With the petals of caresses.

4

After love's conquest, lovers are calm
  And by their women they must rest;
    But these are again possessed
    And shaken by a new desire.

5

  Desire is rising like a lotus through water;
The shooting boughs are bursting with red
                               carelessness;
    The open cups of the buds are ravished
      By drunken bees;
And a man's heart is no different from these.

6

Who could be calm, my darling of the golden voice,
  When every bird sings out his choice?
And each red flower is tipsy with the truth
  Of the wine in the heart of youth?

7

If the grove—that laughs with the white
Teeth of a girl—troubles the anchorite,
    How shall it be with sinners? How?
      Their Paradise is now.

8

What is the soul, weighed down with the wine
   Of the lotus, but a wraith?
      Or faith,
Against red nipples and gold haunches?
   Answer me, divine!

9

Each season be dear to you above
   Past hours of love.
If man has any powers to rise
  When even the flesh seems wise,
  He has it now. He has it now.

Bow down your head, my dear, before the year
　　And the seasons' ring;
　I begin with God, and I fear;
　　But I sing.

THE CLOUD MESSENGER

If I understand Kalidasa at all, underneath THE CLOUD MESSENGER there is a desperate hope. The German "Weltschmerz" is not the same. That is a weariness past all hope; but Kalidasa's is a weariness into belief. George Herbert would have understood.

The most passionate lovers grow tired of the physical act. But what happens when a man exhausts himself, for all his love, of being with God? His 'faith' is no less; his 'belief-belove' is no less. But he asks for a quiet night.

When a man knows the meaning of 'despair', its root and origin, he learns also that 'despair', and 'inspire', and 'Spirit' have the same impulse at their heart as 'respire'.

He breathes again.

THE CLOUD MESSENGER

I

My seeking spirit failed.
                    And in the dark
Of God's white curse I am condemned
To live where loneliness is stemmed
Dark-rooted . . .
                    Under that peak
                              are bathing-places
    Of Shiva with the many faces.

    And heaven is breathing a lark.
Have you not heard the silence speak?

2

I endure under the hills.
                    God bathes here
          In my afternoon and night
            When even the light
          Is a quiet, cool
            Display on the pool,
And fear is the drifting leaves that fall,
   And the flow is nothing,
                    nothing,
                          but yet all.

3

   These heights of the mind.
                    God, will you never know
How I want to blunder, lovingly,
                    below?

4

That monstrous elephant on heat
Can still thrust on towards its sweet
   Delirium ...
               I hear him pound
In a very earthquake on this ground;

                          and yet
   What have I but a golden bracelet?

5

King,
      give me grace if only of a dream.
     My clouded heart,
If it breaks, breaks me apart
In hemispheres of 'is' and 'seems'.

6

I look to the cloud.
                        Oh, not for a shower
        But the birth of a flower,
            And the dew
Of heaven thinking.
                        Is it true,
This darkness of the sky, this I, this I?

7

Build all your life on me.
                            This summer-time
    I send you garlands of sweet hours.
        Have you not prayed
    Quietly, in a temple made
With petal-walls, and heard a prayer
    Your breath, and God's—yet only air?

8

I bend to the rose.
Its silence
Speaks what God above me knows.

9

One flower
A perfect hour;
One breath
And the world's death.

10

I too can sing, my bird.
But if I have a word
From my own breath,
What does it mean but death?
And I've no wing.

This cloud,
and the light behind.
Must I be blind?
My eyes are awake.
I love this world.
Unfold,
White messenger of cloud,
the souled
From the unsouled.

Shapes and shapes torment me.
Changing sky . . .
Must I
Pray to an eternal truth?
Or waste my youth
In a lifetime of desire?
What power in me makes me inquire?

You have a thinking heart;
I have a word—
And on that branch is a bird.

14

If in the darkness I should cry,
What echo can I hear but 'I' and 'I'?

15

And yet I'd shape an other-world.

                                   I'd give

All this that makes me live
   For some enduring flower . . .
I'd live in a stone
If time and change would leave me a minute alone.

16

I dream my God.

                  A greater power than mine
   Awakes to the Divine.

17

But what can *I* do?

                  Ask the petalled rose
—Its sweetness is what ignorance knows.

18

I live in the dark.

                      But you that rejoice in the light
Have never known the splendour of a night.

19

And still I burn with the stars.
I breed like nenuphars
On a cold pool . . .
                I shine.
When one moon-glance of the Divine
Shows me a fool,
Or some bright, witty school
Knows more than in my darkness I dare breathe,
I turn all to belief.
And I believe.

My arrogance is this,
                    not just my earth
        But god-like, my strange miracle of birth.
            The world I'm given . . . Hours
                And the endlessness of flowers.
                    It's true
                That I and you
Must die . . .
                But look for God's sake in a human mind
                And find the shape of God,
                    And find. And find.

I breathe in the air the breath of humankind.
            And my exhausted mind
        Must search, and search, till it grows blind.

But God surrounds me. Darkness is His eyes,
            And the storm His enterprise
        Into my blank of fear . . . And God surrounds me
            Even when I seem alone.
        Help me, my God, to resurrect this bone.

23

Cloud-Messenger, you climb
The fields of the sky, and bring a time
  When travellers' wives can breathe the air,
  And feel the pleasure of disordered hair.

24

Better to kneel in prayer
To Virtue, knowing that the air
    Sighs that you're denied,
      Than on your feet
    Upstanding feel the heat
Of a slow Dullness, merely the fire
      Of everyman's desire.

25

You are the ark where a smouldering soul—
    Shrivelled, understands the whole.
Carry my message, Cloud. Come down like rain
      Not on my trivial pain,
  But on the garden there.
                    The garden there.

I am a burning soul.

                     I reach for the ark

Of your cool body.

               Bless me in the dark.

A cloud surrounds me. My bewildered mind
   Tells me, if I search I find.

                  I find . . .

But in what treasury of love?

                  Alaka—hoard

Of love concealed . . . One kiss, and the adored
        Burns bright

With all my body's, and my soul's delight.

Moon over Shiva,

              in the garden there

Are naked flowers, and now

        Dare I ask how

You prove to me that God Himself is bare?

30

Give me your rose.

                    Give me your sleeping thighs.
  And let birds sing.
             And men be wise.

31

Now in the night I ask who knows
  The saintly budding of the rose.

32

If the grove there laughs, like the white teeth
  Of a girl, with jasmine—and underneath
    His holiness an anchorite is stirred,
    How can a sinner speak an innocent word?

33

I see a rose.

           Its berries are red.
And love, exhausted, hangs his head.

Sing in the darkness.

                     Gold my ears refine
From the ore of your deep meaning's mine;
   Yet even on the surface I assay
Your wealth of heart,
                 eternally, today.

Vapour and light, both wind and water, a cloud—
   Have you not seen them proud
And charged with a message like God's breath?
    They flow through the air.
    They flow.
  And forever, after my private death,
     They'll know.

  How shall I pray?

                Since I must die,
  Better to cry in vain
To the mind's and spirit's goodness than to gain
  A dull content through never asking Why?

37

It moves in light,
                     and even in the dark
     Is an ark
     Half way to heaven.
Cloud-Messenger, lift up my heavy words
      Whether by night or day
        Past the power of birds,
    And tell my God that I have striven.

38

     Caress this mountain crag, and say
        'You are my earth.
     In you was my soul's birth . . .
And Rama,
         Rama,
                day by day
     Mounts you with delight,
      And in the night
   Has only one black fear—
To find that you're not here.'

39

The soft air brings you. Slowly. There
   A rainbird sings his prayer
For your cool showers. And the breeding cranes
Will wait for you with all their delicate grace,
   And even bless you for their pains,
Seeing their white existence reflected in your face.

40

You move across my heaven.
                     You blur my prayer
  Only by being there.

41

And some
      and some
            can worship the peak.
    But can I speak
  In this rare
      and refining air
   Of the mounting feet of God?
                How slowly I
  Climb upward with "Goodbye".

42

I turn to the world,
                and the seasons move
With a God's own truth I cannot prove.

43

I live in faith.
          I hear a quiet rose.
      But I am torn
By something there that grows
  In the mind of a thorn.

44

Yet the wind sits fair,
            and slowly, slowly brings
Your breath within its own.
              A rainbird sings
And its throat is desperate for the showers;
   And among the nodding flowers
    The cranes at breeding-time
Are dancing like white girls in heaven,
    Or poise like the seven
  Stars of the Pleiades.
            And my poor rhyme
  Is an image of these.

45

But leave me now.
                    Better to hope alone
In living flesh than huddle against you
    And feel only bone.

46

Thunder and rain can enrich the the earth;
    The royal swans can dip and sway.
        On the holy lake they sigh
            And pluck the lotus-roots, then fly
            To the icy Himalayas.
                            Why?
    These fellow-pilgrims of my soul
        Need to know the worth
        And the bearing of the Pole.

And some will turn their face to you
    In holy simpleness, and see
       How you and the heavens sweep,
         And cry:
'You'll break the mountains of my earth!
         And I
    Have only this poor valley of my birth.'
      Why should they weep
     For what they're meant to be?
      One 'me' is true.

  But you, Cloud-Messenger, can storm
The ramparts where the elephants guard
    What men declare the 'norm',
And with soft dissolving rain disprove the hard.

48

Indra, Bender of the Bow,
  From a mountain ant-hill in the east
Sends arrowing jewel-rays . . . and now we know
  That blackness of the beast
    Was one of the ways
That Vishnu in a cowherd's rags could hide
  His peacock-splendour.

                              God,

                              the endless-eye'd.

49

Climb the crag of Mala.

                    Even its stone
Is rosy in the dawn.

              And in a countrywoman's eyes
— With their ignorant stare—
  You'll seem a god at sunrise,
    Just by being there.

50

These eyes. Their earthly beauty
          Cries
        That on you rests the duty
Of ploughing. Now!
Come out the god within me.

                          Forth,
And westward, eastward. And then north.

Flood your burning forests. Then
In your weariness look up to Mango's head,
      Cloud-crested.
    When you're rested,
  And your lover's contemplating him instead,
A quiet love will turn to you again.

For the world is God's eternal body. Even I
    See something like Hesperides;
And there the fruit.
                Your nipples.
                    Why
  Is there no glory greater that these
    On the pearling skin of the sky?

53

The woodmen's wives have bowers there.
    You ask me where?
Send down a shower, and then speed on,
      Ignoring
What happens on our human flooring.

54

    The lust of life. This rain
      Again and again;
The flush of apple-blossom in a wind
    And kissing flowers.

And you, Cloud-Messenger, within
      (Not blaming one who sinned)
    Have all the fertile showers . . .
I ask you—yours? or mine the sin?

55

And still the rain, the seed of heaven.
My body drinks.
                    Wild elephants of cloud,
              You breed within me
              As you breed within the rose,
And on the gnarled, fantastic apple-boughs.

        Now nothingness has power
            To fertilize the hour
        When the quiet soul must plead
                    And be
        Not just itself, but even
Only the rain . . .
                    only the rain.

56

    The dappled deer look up and see
        The orange-blossom on the tree,
        Then bend their heads to nuzzle in the sprouts
                Of earth's delight.
                No ecstasy
            But their cool snouts
Are breathing praise to the rain's soft night.

57

If I could travel with a cloud—if I could bear
    The love I have in the highest air,
      You still—being cloud—would pause
        Because . . . because
You come upon a peak.
                (Nor can I speak
  Of my love's altitude, but stay
    And whitely pray).
  I watch the burning bush below,
      And know
Out of this fire you'll make a harvest grow.

58

  Move in the air. You are my day's
      White praise
Of the body's beauty . . . When a mountain stays
    Your drifting pride
    You ride
  A flowering field.
          And in between the birds,
  My airless words.

But when you fill the sky, and your rain
    Turns the leaves over again,
        The holy fig-trees
      (Villages of life)
  Are again awake to the strife
      Of housing crows.
        And I
      Feed these
With my oblation of bread, and pray
    That the wild swan knows
  I have a nesting-ground, for birth
    Of any 'these' and 'those',
Content in love to be their earth.

  But still to a king-town, still
To a capital of love you move in the air,
      And there
        Fulfill
Delight and pain.
          And an out-of-heaven grace
  Touches your reflecting face.

61

You'll not deny me,
                        Cloud, you'll not deny
—After I'm lifted to the sky—
   Exhausted I may lie
And kiss the comeliness of earth,
   And praise the worth
Of a harlot-joy, despised
By all who've never know how you are prized.

62

The jasmine in my garden is white stars.
   Not heaven has so much scent.
I walk alone from the particulars
   Of the absolute within you,
       And invent
Heaven and the jasmine,
             love,
                 myself and you
  Into something new.

63

Crowd your splendour tonight
   In all its white
   Over the gloom
   Of my dark room;
And be reflected in the eyes
—Star-pointed—of my love that lies
And earth-believing in between my thighs.

64

  A bird that sings in the rain . . .
  The river like a girdle flows
Round a sleeping belly of earth,
               and I
Look on her eddying navel; and again
     Reply
With my lipping adoration of the rose.

65

But let your fingers dream among her hair
    And still explore
Those lands of her you knew before
  And yet you wonder 'Where?'

66

And yet those eyes.
    Could I devise
An endlessness of rhyme, I'd not surprise—
    From 'wise'
To the casual question of 'surmise',
    On to the pain that cries
With 'God! God! God!' when a lover dies—
    Truth into lies
In the eternal and returning rhyme of those two eyes.

67

But the morning chatter of birds,
    Is it words? (My words?)
Or do they without meaning sing?
    Are they the ring
Round the ankle of the river flowing
Stumbling over the stones, not knowing
Where she is going, stealing
    Through the dark earth's feeling?
    And who can be wise
    To what a bird cries?

68

The stream is the flow of her hair.
    Not stars, her eyes
Are within their private heaven not divine,
    But shining mine
Make me my own astrologer wise
To know my life and time are fortuned there.

69

But in my darkness, who but I
    Should cry?
But I? ... But I? ... But I? ...
    And who'd know why
    But I?
But I? ... But I ... But I? ...

70

Though all this majesty of stars
    Speaks an eternal truth,
What am I left with, but the scars
    Of my dying youth?
Give me eternity!
               Give me one breath
Through the cold and subtle smiling lips of death.

71

This stone. This temple-shape of life,
    The fabric of our human strife—
        I worship here,
      And still I pray
For one still moment's surcease from the fear
Of even this rose- and birdsong-day.

72

The cranes are flying at the break of day,
        And crying
Faintly like a heart in the sighing air
    —Cool, lotus-scented—
But what does this daylight say
    More than a lover who's lamented
Leaving the limbs he's loved, and bare
        But there,
        Still there?

73

Have you not seen the peacocks dip and sway
      And dance in the light of day?
      But who knows
    When even the eyes of their feathers close
     What I, as well as they,
       Think of a rose?

74

But the dancers have grown tired, and each of the
bells
Round their ankles tells
With a dying sound
That their wrists are weary of the fans.
No man's—
Not a king's delight—
Can offer more than the stillness of the night.

75

Now Shiva's arms—these branching arms of the trees
Uplifted—grip them in the white
And rising crescent of delight . . .
In the smouldering ecstasies
Of sunset, of that western rose,
Answer my questioning prose
With the poems of your stars—

though stars are lees
Of your fermenting wine,
And I drink God within me. Purely mine.

And let the lovers go. Let day's hot lies
    Never contradict the thighs
    That slept and dreamed;
  For the flesh is often wise,
And 'is' deceives more than what 'seemed'.

    And in the pool
    And I that fool
White-faced—the reflection there
    Of nothing staring?
  Or is this troubled water,
             YOU condensed,
My cloud in heaven, and by me sensed,
    The only truth declaring
      Me aware?
  And now this ruffling air!

My image breaks in the water of living.
God,
    God,
        God, what are you giving?

78

Here an answer. Here the lilies are white
On the blackness of the pool. And slight
The woundable and golden fish delight
In darkness.
                    Even praising night.

79

The water is blue, and the wind
Delights to disturb its reticence;
        But not, for God's sake,
        Assaulting the lake,
    But firm with the insolence
Of love and desire . . .
                            And the white
    Cool water-lilies—flowers
        Are the water's living hours.

80

    Bend in the night.
Obscure the shameless light,
    And prove me in the dark
        Either heresiarch
Or love's disciple, prostrate under prayer
    And learning from the sacred air.

81

What God within your Holy Land
   Makes me your believer?

What mind of mine can understand
    Or—Judas—be deceiver?

Now in the dark I see my God
And chastened, I endure the rod.

82

   The world surrounds me.
                  Cloud in heaven,
    Rain down on me the seven
      Human graces . . .

  Let me see them in the faces
    Of the drifting crowd,
And learn, and learn, the unclouded worth
    Of dying man, and God, and earth.

83

Give me a rose, but let its breath
    Sweeten me to death.
  My cloud in heaven, drift in the air
    And whiten my dark earthness everywhere.

84

I have no shape nor life, but drift
    Like heaven's gift
  Over the hills, and feed the streams
    With the offering of my dreams.
     And only then I rain
And worship living things with love and pain.

85

  And still immortal, when I die,
You Messenger in Cloud, will fill the sky
    With more than I
    And yet with "I"
    Still asking why?

But let the quiet hill reply.

86

Now let me go into the night.
   But you, over heaven white,
     Give every blessing
     On a man confessing
Love of the world in a heart that aches
For us and our human sakes.

87

I sing my praise. I sing the eternal air.
   I breathe, I only breathe in prayer.

88

If in the evening God should cry:
   'Who knows?'
What other fool but I
Would answer with a rose?

So I live between two worlds.
                                This subtle earth,
     This flesh, these fireflies in the night
     Are Indra thinking, Shiva in the air . . .
          And you serenely move beyond delight,
          The whiteness of all worth;
And in your 'nothing' fuse the 'now' and 'there'.

My darkness is my hope. The flare of day
     Would tell me what to say,
What see and feel that I *now* know.

     But ignorance is faith. And if I shew
          Nothing in my life to the very end,
               God's darkness will descend,
                    And mine.
               Then darkness is divine.